TEACHERS' POPULATION EDUCATION AWARENESS

TEACHERS' POPULATION EDUCATION AWARENESS

By

Dr. Digumarti Bhaskara Rao
M.Sc., M.A., M.A., M.Ed., Ph.D.,
Reader and Research Director
R.V.R. College of Education
Guntur–522 006
Andhra Pradesh

&

Sheik Johni Basha
M.A., M.Ed.,M.Phil.
Lecturer
R.V.V.N. College
Dharanikota–Amaravathi
Guntur District
Andhra Pradesh

DISCOVERY PUBLISHING HOUSE
NEW DELHI-110002

First Published-2004
Reprinted: 2013

ISBN 81-7141-832-5

Published by
DISCOVERY PUBLISHING HOUSE
4831/24, Ansari Road, Prahlad Street,
Darya Ganj, New Delhi-110002 (India)
Phone: 23279245 • Fax: 91-11-23253475
E-mail:dphtemp@indiatimes.com

Printed at:
Dynamic printers, Delhi

DEDICATED

TO

The Teaching Staff of

Raja Vasireddy Venkatadri Nayudu College

Who Made Us Learn

How to Live Successfully

Dr. Digumarti Bhaskara Rao

Sheik Johni Basha

Preface

Population education is an educational programme which provides for a study of the population situation in family, community, nation and the world with the purpose of developing rational and responsible attitudes and behaviours towards that situation. It is an educational programme that provides for the study of population phenomenon in order to make the students take feasible decisions towards problems arising out of population explosion. The population education needs to be imparted in classrooms effectively by the teachers with adequate awareness about population education.

Identifying the very role of teachers in population education, a study has been undertaken to study the awareness of school teachers about population education. The school teachers are holding high awareness about population education. The men and women teachers, rural and urban teachers, and government and private school teachers are possessing high awareness about population education without any difference between them.

The school teachers should bring in students an adequate awareness about population education and make them settle well in future with small families. This will help the community progress ahead with all amenities.

We are thankful to Asha Bhende, Binod Kumar, Gopala Rao. Hans Raj, Kuppuswamy, Mehta, Pandy, Parakh, Seshadri, Tara Kanitkar and other authors for utilizing their information in preparing this work.

Dr. Digumarti Bhaskara Rao

Sai Soudha
D-43, S.V.N. Colony
Guntur–522 006
Andhra Pradesh
India

Contents

Preface

1. **Introduction** 1-5

Statement of the Problem, Need of the Study, Scope of the Study, Objectives of the Study, Educational Implication

2. **Review of Related Literature** 6-39

Theoretical Perspectives, Problems of Growth Rate of Population, Population Education, Need for Population Education, The Objectives of Population Education, Need and Importance of Curriculum in Population Education, Curriculum of Population Education, Curriculum at the Primary Stage, Why Introduce Population Education at School Stage? Teacher's Role in Population Education, Population Education at Secondary Teachers' Training Level, Teaching Methodologies, Issues, Problems in Implementing Population Education Programmes, Research Studies

3. **Design of the Study** 40-50

Operational Definitions of Key Terms, Population Education, Rural Schools, Urban Schools, Government Schools, Private Schools, Variables of the Study, Rural Versus Urban School Teachers, Government Versus Private School Teachers, Men Versus Women Teachers, Hypotheses of the Study, Hypothesis—1, Hypothesis—2, Hypothesis—3, Hypothesis—4, Selection of Sample, Construction of Research Tool, Administration of the Tool

4. Analysis of Data **51-54**

Hypothesis—1, Hypothesis—2, Hypothesis—3, Hypothesis—4

5. Summary, Conclusions and Discussion **55-60**

Conclusions and Discussion, Suggestions for Further Research

Bibliography *61*

Additional Reading *63*

Index *79*

1

Introduction

Malthus, the famous economist, who in his 'Theory of Population' during the last century, explained that population was increasing in geometric progression whereas production increased in arithmetic progression. He gave a signal warning that the rate of growth of population is high and with all our technological resources at our command, the agriculture and industrial production (regarding essential commodities such as food, clothing, building materials) cannot keep pace with the population growth. His prophecy has come true. We find at present that production, whether in India or in the world, has not been keeping pace with the population growth. The developing nations of the world are bent upon curbing the birth rate through national family planning programmes. The implementation of the small family norm in the minds of the people who have already some fixed traditional values is not an easy task. It requires an understanding of the motivational basis underlying the large-family norm in different cultures. The family planning programme in India has an educational as well as motivational aspect. However, for many reasons, the progress of the family planning programme has not been satisfactory. Attempts are, therefore, being made to bring these people under the fold of a new population philosophy by injecting in them some awareness about the population problem so that they may rationally think about their future and take correct decisions on population matters when the time for such momentous decisions in their lives comes. Hence, a new field of study has been opened which is presently known as 'Population Education', which offers immense possibilities in easing the problem of population, in the long run.

Population education today is one of the important innovations in the area of education. It has spanned through almost the entire spectrum of school education in a relatively short period, and concerted efforts are going on to integrate its elements in other vital sectors of education, namely, non-formal education, adult education and university education. In view of this expansion, a variety of activities relating to different aspects of population education are regularly organised for realising one or the other objective of this endeavour. Since population education is a highly complex area, imbued with cultural sensitivities and regional variations, it has been subjected to varied conceptualisations. Even now, the debate continues regarding its nature vis-a-vis family life education, sex education and family planning. With proliferation of literature on population education and other related areas brought out at international, national and state levels by various organisations and agencies, the non-specialist functionaries find it difficult to comprehend population education in proper perspectives.

In fact, population education is the need of the hour if we want to save ourselves from starvation and extinction. Being of recent origin, a lot of literature has appeared on this topic. Population education, also called "education for population awareness", is of very recent origin.

The population problem being more of a social problem with cultural, economic and political implications, this problem needs to be tackled at the human and individual level. Among all the problems, population education needs to be given top priority. The situation is so grim that something needs to be done quickly and at grassroots level. The younger generation needs to be fully informed and exposed to the dangers of the future. A country where 50 per cent of the population is below 16 years, where marriage is almost universal, where literacy is just 50 per cent, where the standard of living is low and employment is on a dangerous position, population education seems to be most relevant.

Two main reasons for the hidden momentum of population growth in the developing countries are: *(i)* the socio-cultural and religious values of the people which influence their fertility behaviours, and *(ii)* the large young population of these countries. Population change is both a biological as well as a socio-cultural phenomenon. The entire process of reproduction leading to the birth of a child is biological. But the decisions behind the birth of a child and the size of family are governed by socio-cultural values, traditions and customs. For instance, in most of the developing countries, people place a high value on the birth of a son. Similarly there are many other pro-natalist values which influence the fertility behaviour of the people. Generally, socio-cultural values change sluggishly over time through a variety of factors, but one of the most important factors is education. A number of studies show that there is a direct relationship between education of the people and their fertility behaviour. John Knodel and Visid Prachualmoh, in their studies show that the rural women with five or more years of education bore, on an average, just over half as many children as those with no schooling. Urban women with ten or more years of education bore less than 45 per cent as many children as their counterparts with no schooling.

Population education in real sense:

1. Population education is purely an educational programme in order to create awareness and develop understanding. It is neither prescriptive nor directive;
2. The scope of population education is very wide and comprehensive. It includes programmes like sex education, environmental education, family planning programme, etc;
3. Population education is a programme which is meant not only for married couples but also for young pupils

in schools and out of schools and adults. This education programme embraces a large segment of population;

4. Population education programme has adopted many modern innovative techniques to create awareness;
5. The purpose of population education is to study the population phenomenon in a family and community with a view to take decisions;
6. Population education is an exploration of knowledge and attitude about population, the family and sex;
7. Population education is multi-disciplinary in character;
8. It is an educational programme;
9. It is sociological and philosophical in nature.

Statement of the Problem

A study of the awareness about population education among secondary school teachers.

Need of the Study

The world that we live in has changed tremendously. Living is no more pleasant for quite a sizeable section of the mankind, it has turned into a living hell. The population explosion has brought in its trail the most excruciating form of food shortage, unemployment, economic uncertainties, rising incidents of crime and social disorder and environmental pollution. The forewarning of Malthus, more than one and half centuries ago, about the hazards of unplanned population growth has come true in its stark configuration. The demographic trends and traits of the world in its entirety and of our country in particular are quite indicative of the magnitude and intensity of population explosion and its consequent problems.

Over population presents a formidable threat to the survival of a vast segment of the world's population and "its dimensions are as dangerous as a nuclear war". Overwhelming population growth in India brings out the never ending suffering of people. It is creating a serious problem for our national leaders. There is an acute shortage of space in cities. Trees are cut to accommodate more colonies. Deforestation causes pollution and diseases. Monsoons fail. Soil fertility decreases. Thus, the standard of living is affected. Identifying all the problems, the population education is introduced in school education.

To effectively implement the population education in schools, the teachers should have adequate awareness about population education. Identifying the teachers' awareness about population education, this study has been taken up to identify their awareness about population education.

Scope of the Study

The present study aims at the identification of the level of awareness of secondary school teachers about population education and also to compare the awareness level of men and women teachers, rural and urban teachers, and teachers of government and private schools. The study is confined only to the above areas and variables taking the sample from the teachers working in the secondary schools of Guntur district.

Objectives of the Study

The following are the objectives of the present study:

1. To find out the awareness of secondary school teachers about population education;
2. To find out and compare the awareness of rural and urban secondary school teachers about population education;
3. To find out and compare the awareness of the teachers of government and private secondary school about population education;
4. To find out and compare the awareness of men and women teachers about population education.

Educational Implication

The results of this study will help in the effective implementation of the population education programmes in secondary schools.

2

Review of Related Literature

Any worthwhile research in any field of knowledge requires an adequate familiarity with the work which has been already done in the same area. A summary of the writings of recognised authorities and of previous research provides sufficient evidence that the research is familiar with what is already known and what is still unknown. Since effective research bases upon previous knowledge, this step helps to eliminate the duplication of what has been done besides helping in the fixation of useful objectives, formation of appropriate hypotheses, drawing of meaningful conclusions and making commendable suggestions.

The search for related literature is a time consuming process, even then it is necessary for good research. Hence, this chapter is meant for the study and citation of related literature and research studies related to the proposed study on the population education awareness of secondary school teachers.

Theoretical Perspectives

The population explosion is of mammoth dimensions, but it is not the only mammoth problem. It must be set in the context of efforts to bring a decent level of living to the world's poor, and to avoid exhausting the world's resources and polluting the earth's ecosystem in the process.

Population increase leaves its effects on all aspects of man's life—social, political, economic and cultural. There is hardly any sphere of human activity which remains unaffected by population shifts and moments. Our country as a consequence of the exploding population—large scale pollution of the environment, unplanned migration to urban areas in search of gainful employment leading to the creation of urban slums and desertion of villages, increasing poverty, disease social inequalities, ever increasing demand on the nation's limited resources of energy, minerals, land, food—does not need detailed description any more. Today is the identification of suitable strategies to control the galloping population and the will to take serious note of the situation and launch appropriate practical action. Population education is the only desirable solution for it. This approach developing the right type of awareness regarding population situation in the population through education is an important element.

Problems of Growth Rate of Population

1. Growth of population is a hindrance on the path of capital formation, but without capital there can be no economic development. Capital is that part of saving which has been used for productive purposes. For savings, either consumption should be reduced or income increased. Increasing population increases the use of consumption of goods and saving is influenced by various factors, therefore, with increasing population, a developing country cannot think of capital formation. Thus the only way out is capital formation.

2. Increasing population gives birth to food problem. When there is food shortage prices very rapidly go up, with the result that inflationary tendencies begin to gain strength. When prices begin to rise economic imbalances, everywhere, dislocate all plans of development and growth. Many tasks remain unaccomplished. On the other hand, black marketing,

shortages, corruption, strikes, lockouts, labour problems assume seriousness. Economic and political discontentment becomes the order of the day. Obviously, all these activities do not in any way help in economic development of a country.

3. Then another effect of growing population in a developing country is that expenditure goes up very high. Those who are engaged in productive work try to save something for the future as well. Thus there will be a shortage of money in the market and even for meeting day-to-day needs. Thus economic development receives a set back.

4. It is also believed that in a developing country increase in population is bound to result in unemployment. What-so-ever is earned by the people is consumed by them and if at all a part of the income is saved that is taken away by big industrialists to be used in heavy industries. In those countries where a vast majority resides in villages, not much money is available for providing employment to the agriculturists and those engaged in cottage industries. The result is that the pressure of unemployment both in the urban as well as rural areas becomes very heavy.

5. Due to increase in population so many problems arise that even normal development is hindered. Some such problems are vocational and professional institutions like engineering and medical colleges, etc. Economic balance gets disturbed and the circle of poverty and low living standard becomes so wide that it becomes impossible to come out of that. It is most essential that the society should come out of this circle for economic development, but does not find any way out.

6. Population growth also effects adversely the cost of production in developing countries. Both Malthus and Ricardo brought this to focus in their theories.

Population Education

Population education may be defined as an "Educational Programme which provides for a study of the population situation in family, community, nation and the world with the purpose of developing in the students rational and responsible attitudes and behaviour towards that situation". —The Regional Seminar on Population and Family Life Education, UNESCO, Bangkok, 1970.

D.Gopal Rao has suggested the following definition of population education: "Population education may be defined as an educational programme which provides for a study of the population phenomenon so as to enable the students to take rational decisions towards problems arising out of rapid population growth".

Viederman stated that "population education is defined as the process by which the student investigates and explores the nature and meaning of population on process, population characteristics, the causes of population change and consequences of these processes, characteristics and changes for himself, his family, for society and for the world".

According to NCERT, "population education deals with population growth as a phenomenon to be understood for taking decisions about family size and national population policies".

The general conclusions can be drawn from the definitions of population education are:

1. Population education is an educational process to create an awareness in the people regarding causes and consequences of population growth;
2. It creates rational and responsible attitudes and behaviour in the learners about the desirable family size and quality of life;
3. It is multidisciplinary in nature and borrows its contents from disciplines like sociology, anthropology, geography and biology;

4. It refers to the qualitative and quantitative aspects of human population;
5. It provides learning situation for understanding population situation in family, community, nation and world at large;
6. It helps to understand the relationship of man with his environment with due respect to his quality of life;
7. It helps in the implications of population factors for the welfare of the individual, the family and society;
8. Population education implies the nature, causes, changes, characteristics and distribution aspects of human population.

Need for Population Education

Realising the negative effect of rapid population growth on development, many developing countries have launched family planning programmes. The success of family planning programmes in some countries such as China, has been significant in terms of reducing the rate of population growth. However, in a majority of countries, including India, family planning programmes have not been so successful.

There are two main reasons *inter alia* for the hidden momentum of population growth in the developing countries. These are *(i)* The socio-cultural and religious values of the people which influence their fertility behaviour, and *(ii)* The large young population of these countries.

Population change is both a biological as well as a socio-cultural phenomenon. The whole process of reproduction leading to the birth of a child is biological. But the decisions behind the birth of a child and the size of family are governed by socio-cultural values, traditions and customs. For example, in most of the developing countries people place a high value on the birth of a son. Similarly, there are many other pro-natalist values which influence the fertility behaviour of the people. In general socio-cultural values change sluggishly over time through a variety of factors; but one of the most important factors is education. Any coercion in changing the values of the people can backlash and foil all the efforts. There are a number of studies which show a direct relationship between education of the people and their fertility behaviour. For example, a study conducted in Thailand shows that the rural women with five or more years of education bore, on an average, just over half as many children as those with no schooling. Urban women with ten or more years of education bore less than 45 per cent as many children as their counterparts with no schooling.

Similarly, the census data of the Republic of Korea shows that the average number of children born per women among those who studied beyond secondary level was significantly lower (2.15) than among those who never attended school (5.21).

In her inaugural address at the First Conference of Asian Forum of Parliamentarians for Population and Development held at New Delhi from 17 to 20 February 1984, Mrs. Indira Gandhi, the then Prime Minister of India, made a specific reference to the importance of education in inculcating attitudinal and behavioural changes in the people to accept family planning. This should be accompanied by organisational arrangements for contraceptive advice and medical services. She said: "Young people must be in the vanguard of the movement to restrict population growth and to promote sustained development. In schools and colleges and through non-formal education they must be made conscious of the dynamics of population growth and its implications for their own further well being and that of the nation. Properly planned population education programmes need to be introduced at various levels so that when young people marry, they are fully aware of their responsibility to themselves, to future generations and to society. Every occasion and festival, be it religious or otherwise, where people get together, affords excellent opportunity to reach out to them to explain the importance of these programmes".

In view of the potential of its education in alleviating the problems arising from increasing population, many countries have launched population education programmes at different levels of education in both formal and non-formal sectors during the past decade or so.

The following are some other aspects which demand the need of population education:

1. As the population of India is increasing rapidly, its consequences are very harmful for nation's socio-economic development, it is the great need of the hour to inculcate the small family norm in the minds of the children who will become parents tomorrow. It is necessary to provide the factual information for this;
2. The students in high schools and colleges need to be taught the physiology of reproduction. It will not be difficult for them to understand the idea of the whole phenomenon of human reproduction. Knowledge about the human reproductive system can be imparted to them;
3. In the villages, it is difficult to measure the population trends, the education for population awareness will emphasis the proper registration of births and deaths of the people;
4. Population education should emphasis the fact that the growth of population must be zero. Birth control is not unnatural;
5. Stephen Viederman has pointed out that "The aims of education are to increase awareness and hopefully to help us achieved wisdom in the conduct of our lives, both as individuals and collectively. These aims are shared by the new field to be called population awareness education—population education at the result of the knowledge and understanding achieved through their education, make responsible decisions concerning their own reproductive behaviour. The key concept is responsible decision making which involves for knowledge and understanding of the consequences of one is own actions. This is the beginning of wisdom

and represents the moral and ethical purpose of population education".

The Components of Population Education

There are three major components of population education, viz., *(i)* Determinants of population growth, *(ii)* Consequences of population growth, and *(iii)* Population control.

(i) ***Determinants of Population Growth:*** Here it is necessary to point out the causes or determinants of population growth. The factors which motivate people towards their population decision are very complex. Some of them are connected with traditions and culture of the particular place; some of them are concerned with religious and superstitious beliefs. In some societies, the people like to bring up the large families. Some believe that children are the gifts of God. So they are in favour of large families of sons and grandsons.

(ii) ***Consequences of Population Growth:*** The consequences of population growth are the most important element of population education programme of the world over. This factor has directly effected the individuals as well as the nations. Consequences of rapid population growth on economic and social development, employment opportunities, food, health, nutrition, housing, education, etc., have become the important component of population education.

(iii) ***Population Control:*** The third component of population education is the population control. Though population education cannot control population growth directly like the family planning but it seeks to make pupils understand that a planned small family is more desirable if national and personal development are so desired.

The Objectives of Population Education

The national twin workshops held at Srinagar and Pune in the second and third weeks of July 1980 respectively unanimously endorsed what Dr. V.K.R.V. Rao had stated in Bombay seminar. The theme of the twin workshops was "Population Education: Tasks and Challenges". These workshops were organised for key persons, policy makers and executives responsible for planning, launching and implementing population education projects in the ten states that volunteered to join the National Population Education Project in its first phase.

The objectives of population education should be to enable students to understand:

(i) that family size is controllable;

(ii) that population limitation can facilitate the development of a higher quality of life in the nation; and

(iii) that a small family size can contribute materially to the quality of living for the individual family.

The National Population Education Project document states the long range objectives of the project categorically as follows:

The primary goal of the project is to gear the entire educational system in the country to the realisation of the potential role of education in the development efforts of the country, and of inter-relationships between population situation and different aspects of the quality of life at the micro and macro levels. The firm's long range objectives of the programmes are:

(i) to help students develop an insight into interrelationships between population growth and the process of social and economic development at the individual, family, society, national and international levels;

(ii) to make children and teachers aware of the population situation in the country and the targets and efforts of the Govt. of India in solving this problem;

(iii) to institutionalise population education in the formal education system, including universities and non-

formal education programmes at the national and state levels; and

(iv) to develop desirable attitudes and behaviour in teachers and students as well as the community at large towards population issues so that they may take rational decisions about their family size and the quality of life that they would like to have.

Need and Importance of Curriculum in Population Education

In a dynamic society, the curriculum of educational institution is subject to modification from time to time. In each educational process the three basic components are inseparable such as the teacher, the learner and the curriculum. A concept of curriculum is more helpful and valuable than a formal definition because of the diversity of curriculum practices, programmes and interpretations throughout India.

Curriculum should be considered as an epitome of the rounded hole of the knowledge and experiences of human race. The curriculum of population education includes the learners' experiences in or outside the school that are included in a programme which has been divided to help him develop mentally, physically, emotionally and morally.

The teacher in the population education programme is required to achieve the prefixed aims and objectives. For the purpose he has to employ suitable instructional methods and procedures. But this he can do only when he knows what effects he is to make and in what order. In other words, he should know the content of population education curriculum which consists of subjects, activities and experiences in a properly graded form. Curriculum is in fact the "Warp and Woof" of the whole educational process.

The need and importance of curriculum in population education may be summed up as follows:

1. ***Achievement of Aims:*** Merely defining the aims of population education is futile. There should be well-planned efforts and organisations to achieve the aims

of population education. We must think of knowledge, activities, experiences and other influences which help in the achievement of aims of population education;

2. ***Criteria for Suitable Teachers:*** It is the curriculum which can show what type of teachers are required for these new types of educational systems. We should know what type of work they are required to do and this should be according to the requirements of the curriculum;

3. ***Selection of Suitable Methods:*** The curriculum of population education enables the teacher to select suitable methods of teaching. "How to teach" will be determined by what to teach;

4. ***Reflects Trends in Education:*** The curriculum is the means to achieve the aims of population education which are dynamic and go on changing with the changing social requirements. Naturally, the curriculum will reflect the trends and growth of population in education.

Curriculum of Population Education

One of the basic principles of education is that educational matter presented to the child should be at his level of understanding. The curriculum constructors should always have in their minds this important fact while planning the curriculum. Population education cannot, at all, be an exception to these. Having fixed the content of population education, the next step is to find out what type of content in which stage, so that the objectives of population education can be achieved.

(A) Curriculum at the Primary Stage

Primary education is considered as the foundation on which the superstructure of higher education stands. The pupils at this stage are small and growing. The curriculum is to be arranged in accordance with their age, need, growth, development and interest. The curriculum at the primary stage cannot be equivalent with that of the secondary stage. The population education curriculum at the primary stage can be categorised under important headings:

1. Social Life

(i) Population growth and its social causes

(ii) Population growth and superstitions

(iii) Population growth and standard of life

(iv) Population growth and social disharmony

(v) Population growth and beggar problem in India

(vi) Population growth and lack of discipline

(vii) Disadvantages of early marriage

(viii) Rapid growth in population and its impact on the socio-economic life.

2. Economic Life

(i) Population growth and food problem

(ii) Population growth and less per capita income

(iii) Population growth and unemployment

(iv) Population growth and less availability of consumer goods

(v) Education and employment of women

(vi) Scarcity of means and vastness of demand.

3. Environment

(i) Population growth and air pollution

(ii) Pollution growth and water pollution

(iii) Population growth and soil pollution

(iv) Population growth and noise pollution

(v) Population growth and its pressure on soil, water, air and sound pollution, deforestation, soil erosion and threat to wild life

(vi) Population growth and natural calamities.

4. Family Life

Parents and their role in family life:

(i) Population growth and marriage

(ii) Population growth and remarriage

(iii) Population growth and universality of marriage

(iv) Population growth and belief in such norms as "Child is the gift of God"

(v) Population growth and family tensions

(vi) Population growth and lack of care, love and affection

(vii) Population growth and low standard of living

(viii) A daughter is an important as the son. Small-size family is needed for a better quality of life. Large-size family results in adverse impact on the health of mother and child.

5. Health

(i) Population growth and diseases

(ii) Population growth and poor quality of medical facilities

(iii) Population growth and shortage of medicines

(iv) Population growth and shortage of doctors

(v) Cleanliness, safe drinking water, balanced diet and health facilities

(vi) Healthy mother, healthy child need to have fewer children.

6. Nutrition

(i) Population growth and low quality food

(ii) Population growth and adulteration

(iii) Population growth and lack of nutritious food

(*iv*) Population growth and hunger.

7. Educational Life

(*i*) Population growth and poor quality of education

(*ii*) Population growth and over-crowded classes

(*iii*) Population growth and shortage of schools and colleges

(*iv*) Population growth and shortage of efficient teachers

(*v*) Population growth and illiteracy.

8. Demographic Implications

(*i*) Population dynamics

(*ii*) Size, structure and composition of population at local and national level

(*iii*) Causes and consequences of population growth

(*iv*) Impact of migration to rural and urban areas.

(B) Curriculum at the Secondary Stage

Children at the secondary stage are much more mature and grown-up in comparison to the primary school children. The curriculum at the secondary stage should be arranged and constructed keeping in view the growth and development, age, maturation and interest of the children. The period of adolescence starts at this stage for which a number of points will have to be taken into consideration, while framing the curriculum.

The curriculum at the secondary stage can be divided into the following headings:

1. Social Life

(*i*) Marriage—types and necessity

(*ii*) Effect of divorce

(*iii*) Unscientific explanation of prejudices and social tradition

- *(iv)* Population growth and disharmony
- *(v)* Role of women in social and national development
- *(vi)* Population growth and quality of life
- *(vii)* Interrelationship between various aspects of marriage and quality of life.

2. Economic Life

- *(i)* Population growth and per capita income
- *(ii)* Population growth and economic life
- *(iii)* Demand and production
- *(iv)* Population growth and price rise
- *(v)* Population growth and national income
- *(vi)* Population growth and unemployment
- *(vii)* Population growth and lack of industrialisation
- *(viii)* Population growth and labour supply.

3. Demographic Implication

- *(i)* Mortality, fertility and migration
- *(ii)* Population policy
- *(iii)* Birth rate and death rate
- *(iv)* Methods of family planning
- *(v)* Estimation of world population in general and population of India in specific
- *(vi)* Population growth in developed and developing regions of the world
- *(vii)* Occupational structure of India.

4. Sex Life

- *(i)* Sex education
- *(ii)* Concept of sex deviations
- *(iii)* AIDS—causes, symptoms and prevention

(iv) Sex mechanism

(v) Physiology and hygiene of human reproduction

(vi) Structure, type and functions of different glands

(vii) Basic knowledge about different sexual diseases like VD, STD, etc.

5. Environmental Life

(i) Environmental pollutions like water, air, noise, soil, etc.

(ii) Adulteration of food materials

(iii) Control of environmental pollution

(iv) Environmental pollution and its effects on human life

(v) Better environment for better living

6. Family Life

(i) Concept and type of family

(ii) Merits and demerits of joint family system

(iii) Origin of the family

(iv) Small size family and large size family, a comparative picture

(v) Government benefits for green-card holders.

Why Introduce Population Education at School Stage?

There are a number of plausible reasons for imparting population education to young children. Some of these are commonly recognised in most of the developing nations, though there are some that have specific relevance to the Indian situation. The following compelling reasons merit our attention:

(i) Since about 42 per cent of the Indian population consists of children below the age of fifteen years and their number is swelling enormously because of the rapid population growth, their role will be crucial in shaping the population situation of the country in immediate future. At present as many as ten million out of this age-group are entering into parenthood every year. If they are made properly aware about critical dimensions of population phenomena, they can be expected to take informed and rational decisions regarding population issues;

(ii) It is generally observed that the perception of population—related issues by an individual may vary from that desired by the community or defined by national policies. This so happens because the national policies in respect of population issues are formulated according to the needs and requirements of the well-defined national goals, whereas individuals perceive the population phenomena in their own socio-cultural milieu shaped by the traditional norms and value patterns. Unless a perceptible social change directed towards the attainment of national goals takes place, there cannot be commonality in the patterns of perception at individual, community and national levels. With a view to inducing such a social change, education can play a decisive role;

(iii) The purpose of education is to prepare the young for adult life. This requires both presenting relevant information and teaching analytical process and skills that can be broadly applied. Since population affects all aspects of modern life, important population issues and methods for analysing population problems should be an integral part of in-school education;

(iv) Population issues are predominantly value laden. Individual decisions invariably influenced by the value orientation of individuals are shaped by their socialisation process. Attitude in particular are formed during the early age of a person. The intervention of population education at school stage can therefore prove very effective, as it would provide suitable setting for values and clarification and development of scientific temper;

(v) The whole business of family planning and reduction of birth rate is not "once-for-all" affair, nor it is concerned only with the currently fertile population that is capable of adding the country's numbers. Even as eternal vigilance is the price we have to pay for liberty, similarly, family planning education and programmes have to be on a continuous basis. It is here that population education becomes relevant as a motivational instrument that will inject these new entrants with the desire to adopt family planning as a way of life;

(vi) It is also obvious that population education must cover not only the college going students but those who only go to schools, as majority of children grow into adulthood without having more than secondary and in many cases only primary education;

(vii) At times, it is argued that since population related topics have always been in textbooks, particularly of social studies, economics, geography, biology or home economics, there is no need to introduce population education. However, the topics in the existing textbooks have generally been treated in a neutral manner and invariably as facts to be memorized rather than to be treated as tools for sound decision-making. It is by conscious efforts through population education that the existing contents could be reoriented and reinforced in order to realise the desired objectives of population education;

(viii) It is hoped that the integration of population education elements into the existing education system would encourage the children who would grow adults while passing through the school stage, to play the role of opinion leaders in their respective communities. They may help in preparing a congenial atmosphere in the community for the realisation of national demographic and development goals;

(ix) It is also expected that population education would eventually make the learners realise that although it is essential to believe in the dignity of the individual and freedom of choice, but it is equally important to dovetail the belief with the social good and national demands.

Teacher's Role in Population Education

The teacher has to play several roles such as:

— Teacher as an agent for social change

— Teacher's faith in national development through proper planning

— Teacher's conviction and basic belief in the need for checking further growth in population

— Teacher's faith in education as a strong tool of social change and development

— Teacher's firm belief in population education programme as a sound measure to achieve national goals

— Teacher's knowledge of population education areas

— Teacher's basic understanding about population education concept

— Teacher's knowledge of socio-economic problems of the country

— Teacher's knowledge of sex and human reproduction system and its relation to social function of life

— Teacher's skill in discriminating information according to age and intellectual capacity of students

— Teacher's characteristics, e.g., being intelligent, liberal, creative, imaginative, innovative and interested in social needs and problems.

Population Education at Secondary Teachers' Training Level

Development of the right type of awareness of the population problem and the inculcation of rational attitude and responsible behaviour in the young towards the population situation cannot be effectively realised if the classroom teacher is found wanting in these very qualities. If the teacher is to act as a change agent for effecting desirable changes in the awareness, attitude and behaviour of his pupils, it is imperative that he should keep himself atleast of the population situation with all its attendant consequences. It is in this context that population education has relevance for teacher training programmes. In other words, population education should be an integral part of teacher training at different levels of teacher preparation. The content of population education at different levels of teacher training should invariably include all areas of knowledge of population education which are to form the content for students at different levels of schooling.

The content of population education should be determined by the objectives which it seeks to achieve. The following are the objectives of population education for teacher training at the secondary level:

1. To create an awareness of the population problem, with reference to India in particular and the world in general;
2. To develop an understanding of the impact of population growth on the various aspects of human life: physical and mental, social and cultural, moral and ethical, economical and political;
3. To develop an understanding of the ways and means of controlling population growth;
4. To develop an understanding of the population policies and programmes of India;
5. To develop an understanding of the meaning, scope and importance of population education;
6. To develop skill in collecting and interpreting demographic data;
7. To develop skill in integrating elements of population education in various curricular and co-curricular activities;

8. To develop positive attitude towards implementation of population education programmes in school;
9. To develop the skill of evaluating student learning in population education.

These objectives of population education can be realised through a well planned curriculum in population education for secondary teacher training course.

Teaching Methodologies

There are a good number of methods, both formal and informal, to spread the message of population education. Population education curriculum should be arranged accordingly to introduce sufficient by the topics, stories plays and co-curriculum activities based on practical life of the children. Textbooks should be written in simple language with illustrations and pictures to cater to the interests of the children. The teachers are free to adopt not any single method but a combination of methods as and when required, depending on the target.

1. ***Classroom Teaching:*** In this method, the teacher should take some classes on population education to enable the students to develop a consciousness to the problems we face due to rapid population growth. The students must get some knowledge about consequences and remedial measures of population growth. The students will be acquainted with the government policies to control rapid population growth.
2. ***Extra Moral Lectures:*** Experts from different fields such as family planning, economics, sociology, anthropology, geography, political science, may be invited to the schools to deliver talks such as—problems of population growth, causes of population growth, effects of over population, family planning and welfare, problem of unemployment and population education and sex education.

3. ***Organisation of Co-curricular Activities:*** The teachers may organise suitable co-curricular activities based on the theme of population education programmes such as—debates and essay competitions, poetry, short plays, one-act plays and seminars, folk programmes like folk dances, folk dances etc., can be arranged. These competitions may be organised among the children of the same school and other schools. Such competitions may also be held at the circle level and the district level.

4. ***Creative Writings Among Teachers:*** School teachers may write stories, plays and other creative writings in various forms to suit the children. For the best writers, attractive prizes should be awarded.

5. ***Display of Posters:*** Posters, pictures, charts, maps and pamphlets based on population education should be displayed on the walls of classrooms, common room and corridors.

6. ***Wall Magazine:*** Both students and teachers may display poems, short stories and paper cuttings on population problems on the wall magazine of the school.

7. ***Visits and Field Trips:*** Students under the supervision of teachers may be taken on visits and field trips to family planning centres to get some information about the methods of family control.

8. ***Film Shows:*** Film shows may be organised in the school to give some message on the evils of large family size in rural areas and over-crowing in urban areas.

Issues

Some issues related to methodologies of teaching in population education are:

— Which are the appropriate and effective methods of teaching population education?

— What is the possibility of using discovery or inquiry approach in teaching population education in view of the existing situations in schools?

— Isn't it a contradiction to expect teachers to use the discovery or problem—solving approach when they use traditional methods of teaching the subjects into which population education has been integrated?

Problems in Implementing Population Education Programmes

A close look at population education programme in Asia and the Pacific region reveals that, although, some of these national programmes are decades old, they have a long way to go before it can be said that population education is fully institutionalised in their education systems. Most of them are still passing through a transition period. This is because of the number of problems of curriculum, integration in textbooks, training of teachers and other personnel, etc. Some problems in implementing and integrating population education in school levels can be highlighted such as:

1. Lack of commitment
2. Lack of planning and co-ordination
3. Lack of resources
4. Religious taboos
5. Inadequate curriculum and material development
6. Problems of variety of languages and dialects
7. Lack of transport and communication
8. Inadequate encouragement for period having small families
9. Lack of trained teachers
10. Problem of integration
11. Lack of suitable literature

In connection with the introduction of population education into the school curriculum, note will have to be taken of:

(a) the views of parents regarding the advisability or the appropriateness of including certain topics;

(b) the preparation of teachers to handle population education;

(c) the age levels at which different topics should be introduced, and the key concepts to be emphasised at each age level;

(d) the subject matter areas through which the topics, and the key concepts involved in them, could be introduced;

(e) the lack of relevant research data, especially on the motivational issues.

Research Studies

Due to the shortage of time and resources, some of the important studies related to this study are quoted here in a different manner.

K. Balasubramaniam and Others—A Study of the Reactions of High School Teachers to Population Education as Integral Part of Curriculum

Findings

1. A very high awareness of the population problem in India was found amongst teachers. The teachers replied that unemployment, low standard of living and food shortage were due to over population.
2. Most of the teachers were not aware of the efforts being made to introduce population education in school curricula. They did not know about the national seminar on population education held at Bombay in August 1969.
3. Most of the teachers were of the opinion that population education should be introduced in school curricula. The suggested contents are: *(i)* Relationship between economic growth and population, *(ii)* Ways and means of finding solutions to population problem,

and *(iii)* Demographic trends of population growth. However 30 per cent teachers who did not approve of the inclusion of population education in the school curricula, were of the opinion that immaturity of students at school level would act as a barrier to teaching the subject.

4. Majority of the teachers were of the opinion that sex education should be taught along with population education. They felt that it would help in removing wrong ideas and build up the moral character of students.

5. Whereas only 23 per cent of teachers were of the opinion that population education should be taught as a separate subject, but 49 per cent of the teachers felt that it should be integrated with other subjects.

P.V. Varghese—A Study of the Attitude of Teachers towards Different Aspects of Population Education

Findings

1. The teachers teaching in the primary and high school levels differed in their attitude towards population education.

2. The male and female teachers differed in their attitude towards population education.

3. Marital status of teachers had no bearing on the attitude towards population education.

4. Teachers belonging to different religious groups did not differ in their attitude towards population education.

5. The male and female teachers differed in their opinion towards sex education.

6. The teachers belonging to different religious differed in their attitude towards sex education.

7. Marital status of teachers was not related to their attitude to sex education.

8. Whereas the religion of teachers was significantly related to their attitude to family planning and sex education, it was not related to their attitude towards population education.

J.R. Maheswari—A Study of the Receptiveness of School Teachers to Population Education

Findings

1. The teachers had very high awareness of the population problem that the country and the world is facing.

2. About 92 per cent of the teachers said that unemployment and poor standard of living were mainly due to over population.

3. Eighty per cent of the teachers agreed that a small family is advantageous; 40 per cent of them expressed that it enables the people to have higher standard of living; 24 per cent said that it leads to a happy, comfortable life.

4. Majority of teachers preferred two sons and only one daughter.

5. The majority of teachers did not believe in the effectiveness of population education at school level. They felt that adults should be educated in the philosophy and practice of family planning.

6. About 60 per cent of the teachers did not know the efforts being done to introduce population education in schools.

7. The teachers were of the opinion that topics such as the characteristics, causes and trends of population growth, its impact on the economic and social development of the country, and also on the health and nutrition of people, and the knowledge about family life should be included in a course on population education.

8. Eighty three per cent of the teachers agreed that anatomy and physiology of human reproduction should form a part of population education. However, they were against introducing sex education in schools.
9. A majority of teachers favoured the idea of integrating population education concepts, with existing school subjects. They felt that most of the concepts could be integrated through social studies, sciences, languages and mathematics.

N.N. Srivastava—A Study of the Knowledge and Attitude of Teachers Towards the Introduction of Population Education in School Curricula

Findings

1. Majority of teachers were aware of the population problem.
2. The consequences of over population in their opinion were unemployment, under employment and low standard of living.
3. The majority of teachers felt that if the growth of population is not checked, the economic development of the country will be hampered.
4. Most of the teachers suggested that the best way of checking over population is by educating the younger generation.
5. Majority of the teachers commended a family size up to four children, out of which at least two should be sons.
6. Most of the teachers were of the opinion that population education should form a part of school education, only at the university stage. Majority of the teachers were of the opinion that it should be integrated with existing school subjects especially through social studies course.

7. Majority of the teachers felt that the course should be a subject for annual examination.

Shailbala Dayal—Knowledge of School Teachers about Family Planning and Their Reaction to Population Education Curriculum

Findings

1. A majority of male as well as female teachers (90 per cent male and 75 per cent female) favoured a two to four years interval between two births.
2. About 75 per cent of teachers thought it desirable to use methods to prevent unwanted pregnancies.
3. All female married teachers approved the use of family planning methods only after one or two children.
4. While about 65 per cent of the teachers wanted the concept of small family and its advantages be taught to the high school children, only 24 per cent thought it necessary for students at the elementary level.
5. While about 55 per cent of the teachers recommended the teaching of trends in population growth, birth and migration be taught at the high school level, only six per cent of teachers thought it suitable for the elementary level and 17 per cent of teachers thought it suitable for the middle school level.
6. While 67.6 per cent teachers recommended that government policy and programme of population control be taught at the high school level, they did not want this topic to be taught at the elementary level.
7. While 50 per cent of the teachers thought that physiology of human reproduction could be taught at the higher secondary level, none of the teachers wanted this to be taught at the primary level and only 7 per cent of the teachers felt that the topic is suitable for the middle school level.

8. While 70 per cent of the teachers recommended that population education should be integrated with social studies, 30 per cent wanted it to be integrated with biological sciences and 24 per cent favoured its integration with civics and economics.

Ganesh Lal Mehta—A Study of the Opinion of Parents and Teachers Towards Introduction of Population Education in High Schools of Bhubaneswar.

Findings

1. The teachers and parents irrespective of their sex and educational background had a favourable opinion towards inclusion of population contents in the education programme. They recommended the inclusion of demographic concepts, economic and social consequences of population growth and the process of human reproduction in the curriculum.
2. Both the teachers and parents however felt that agencies other than schools are more suitable to teaching of population education.
3. The teachers and parents irrespective of sex differences or income and educational background have expressed the opinion against the teaching of human reproduction in schools.
4. The teachers and parents were of the opinion that population education will help in creating right attitude towards small family size. However, parents from high income group were more favourably inclined towards this view than middle income parents. Parents of the low income group were strongly opposed to this opinion.
5. While parents were optimistic that the concept of a small family is not only desirable but also achievable through population education, the teachers in general did not agree with this opinion.

S.L. Nagda, et.al,—A Study of the Opinion of Teachers Towards Population Education

Findings

1. Ninety per cent of the sample teachers knew the meaning of population education.
2. Sixty per cent felt that population education and family planning are one and the same.
3. Twenty five per cent of the teachers considered population awareness and planned parenthood as a part of population education.
4. Ninety per cent felt that population education is necessary for the youth for responsible parenthood.
5. Fifty per cent of respondents considered that the standard of living is not affected by the size of family.
6. About 90 per cent felt that the size of the family can be planned by all human beings.
7. Most of the respondents agreed that too many children would affect the health of the mother and that spacing of children is necessary for maintaining the health of the mother.
8. Most of the respondents were of the opinion, that a small family norm is necessary to lead a happy and comfortable life.
9. A majority of the respondents agreed that our country cannot meet the needs of its people if the rate of growth of population remains the same.
10. Most of the respondents felt that population education would develop right attitudes concerning family life among younger generation.
11. Ninety per cent considered that late marriage is one of the methods of controlling family size.
12. Sixty per cent thought that over population leads to economic and social instability in the country.

13. Most of the respondents felt that it is necessary to impart knowledge on human reproduction and nutrition to our masses.

14. Regarding the methodology to be adopted for creating population awareness among the community, 50 per cent considered exhibitions and film shows as appropriate methods where as 30 per cent considered lectures by experts and group discussions as appropriate methods.

Ramachandran—A Study of the Knowledge and Attitude of Teachers of Kurnool Towards Population Education

Findings

1. At the beginning of the course, 40 per cent of the participants were not aware of the meaning of population education. At the end of the course, most of them had better concept of population education.

2. In the pre-test, 40 per cent of the participants considered population awareness programme as a part of family planning propaganda. In the final test, about 80 per cent of the participants considered that population awareness is also a part of population education.

3. Whereas in the pre-test only 25 per cent of the participants could trace the relationship of family, food and nutrition and planned parenthood to population education, and in post-test more than 75 per cent of the participants could adequately explain the relationship.

4. Before the course, about 60 per cent of the participants considered that family planning and population education are one and the same. But after the course, most of the participants considered that family planning and population education are not one and the same.

5. In the pre-test, 20 per cent of the participants disagreed that the size of the family cannot be controlled by human beings. In the post-test most of them thought that size of the family can be controlled.
6. In the pre-test, 50 per cent of the participants considered that there is no proper environment in schools and colleges for creating population awareness among students. In the post-test, more than 70 per cent of the participants considered that it is possible to create awareness of population problem in the students by a programme of lecture by experts and by organising film shows and exhibitions.
7. About 65 per cent of the participants considered late marriage as one the methods for controlling the family size.
8. Majority of the participants both in the pre-test and post-test considered that over-population leads to economic and social instability in the country.
9. Majority of participants (both in the pre-test and post-test) opined that it is necessary for our country to check its population growth and also it is necessary to impart knowledge on human reproduction and nutrition to our masses.
10. Majority of the participants considered that a small family is conductive to higher standard of living and that population education is necessary for developing responsible parenthood among the youths.
11. All the participants considered that spacing of child births is necessary for the health of the mother and for the health and happiness of children.
12. Both in the pre and post tests, there was agreement among the participants that sex education in the context of population is necessary to eliminate some mis-conceptions about human reproduction in the younger generation.

D.Gopal Rao—A Study of the Awareness of Teachers on Population Problems and their Reaction to the Introduction of Population Education in Schools

Findings

1. Majority of the teachers had a good knowledge of the causes and consequences of over population.
2. They ascribed unemployment, food shortage and poverty to over-population in the country.
3. They favoured the introduction of population education in schools.
4. Most of the teachers felt that it should be taught as an integral part of the school curriculum.
5. They recommended that it should be made compulsory in schools and also be an examination subject.
6. They also favoured the teaching of sex education in schools.

N.V. Vaswani and Indira Kapoor—School Teachers Attitude Towards Population Education

Findings

1. While 54.2 per cent teachers had heard about population education, only about 3 per cent teachers could give somewhat correct meaning of the word population education.
2. When the meaning and scope of population education was made clear about 75 per cent of teachers felt that it should be introduced as a subject in the school curriculum.
3. The teachers who were not in favour of introducing the subject felt that the subject was difficult for the teachers to teach and for the pupils to understand.
4. While 47.2 per cent teachers felt that population education should be integrated with other school

subjects, 8.7 per cent teachers felt that it should be taught as a separate subject and 13.9 per cent teachers did not express their opinion.

5. Nearly 49 per cent of teachers were of the opinion that it should be taught earlier than eighth standard and only 26.6 per cent felt that it should be introduced at the college level.

6. Nearly 44 per cent of teachers preferred not to teach this subject as they were not qualified to do so.

Rashmin, Thakore—Developing a Curriculum in Population Education for Secondary Teacher Under Training

Findings

Though the study was mainly concerned with developing a curriculum, it has also reflected the method of implementing the programme. It was found that the ten topics included in the model can be taught in 20 periods of 40 minutes each, thus covering each topic in two periods. It has also revealed that another 10 periods are required for imparting the message through co-curricular activities. Thus the programme can be covered in 30 periods of 40 minutes duration spread over in an academic year.

The research studies and the related literature gave a scope for the present study on the awareness about population education of secondary school teachers.

3

Design of the Study

Planning is a necessary step for a good research. Design is the heart of any research. In this chapter, the following aspects have been discussed which are concerned with the design of the present study. Research procedures followed include the operational definitions different terms used, the various hypotheses that were framed for verification and the rationale of these hypotheses. Selection of the sample includes the sampling techniques used, the reasons for selection of a particular sampling technique and the selection of sample according to different variables. Selection research tools includes selection of suitable tool for collection of data, description of tool selected, testing its suitability for the present study and the procedure followed in the administration of the tool to collect the data required for this study.

OPERATIONAL DEFINITIONS OF KEY TERMS

The operational definitions of the important terms used in the present study are given here under.

Population Education

Population education is an educational programme which provides for a study of the population situation in family, community, nation and the world with the purpose of developing rational and responsible attitudes and behaviour towards that situation.

Rural Schools

The schools located in rural areas (panchayat villages) were considered as rural schools.

Urban Schools

The schools located in urban areas (municipalities and corporations) were considered as urban schools.

Government Schools

The schools under the sole management of government officials are government schools. The schools managed by the Zilla Parishads, Municipalities and Government were included in this category.

Private Schools

The schools managed by private organisations or individuals, either partially or totally, are private schools. The public schools, the government recognised and aided schools were included in this category.

VARIABLES OF THE STUDY

The variables are the conditions or characteristics that a researcher manipulates, controls or observes. The variables may be abstractions that can not be observed. These variables must be defined operationally by describing some samples of actual behaviour that are concrete enough to be observed directly. The relationship between these observable incidents may be deduced as consistent or inconsistent with the consequences of the hypothesis. Thus, the hypothesis may be judged to be probably true or probably false. Variables are a necessary requisite for any worthwhile research for the purpose of comparison.

The variables considered for the present study were rural versus urban teachers, government versus private school teachers and men versus women teachers. The rationale for choosing the above stated variables is discussed here with.

Rural Versus Urban School Teachers

Locality was taken as a variable to see if there is any significant difference between rural and urban school teachers in possessing population education awareness. As the living conditions, facilities of the schools, knowledge of the general issues, etc., there may be a difference between rural and urban school teachers in the possession of population education awareness. So, a comparison of rural and urban school teachers will reveal the difference in awareness in any exists in the sub-samples.

Government Versus Private School Teachers

The exposure of teachers to the management, salaries, co-operation, etc., will differ significantly in private schools and government schools. The facilities available and the working conditions also differ significantly in private and government schools. So, it is important to study about the difference in the awareness about population education possessed by the teachers teaching in government and private secondary schools.

Men Versus Women Teachers

The physical characteristics, the mental maturity, the exposure to the society, the social taboos, the societal status, the initiativeness, etc., vary significantly when compared men and women teachers. So, the gender variable is selected to find out the awareness about population education.

HYPOTHESES OF THE STUDY

Hypothesis are the tentative conclusions for verification. The hypotheses were stated in null form. A null hypothesis states that there is no significant difference or relationship between two or more variables. It concerns to a judgement as to whether apparent differences or relationships are true differences or relationships or whether they merely result from sampling errors.

The following hypotheses were formulated based on the variables and objectives of the study.

Hypothesis—1

There is no high awareness about population education among secondary school teachers.

Hypothesis—2

There is no significant difference in the awareness of teachers of rural and urban secondary schools about population education.

Hypothesis—3

There is no significant difference in the awareness of teachers of government and private secondary schools about population education.

Hypothesis—4

There is no significant difference in the awareness of men and women teachers about population education.

SELECTION OF SAMPLE

After finalizing the variables of the present study, consideration was given to whether the entire population is to be made the subject for data collection or a particular group is to be selected as representative of the whole population. The 'entire population' here refers to all the teachers teaching in secondary schools of Guntur district.

Of the above two techniques, the selection of a group as a representative of the whole population was found to be more convenient and suitable. The technique leads to a considerable save of time, effort and finance. The number of teachers selected will be small, and so it is possible to make a detailed and intensive study. This generally leads to more accurate and reliable results.

In any social research, various methods are utilized for selection and drawing of samples. After a detailed study of all these methods, and considering the variables selected for the research work, the 'stratified sampling technique' was found to be most suitable.

In the stratified sampling method, the entire population will be divided into smaller homogeneous groups or strata, and then a sample is selected within each group. Every sampling unit in the population is placed in one of the strata prior to the selection of the sample so that the sum of the strata is identical with the population.

In the stratified sampling method, the investigator has greater control over the selection of the sample when compared with random sampling. In random sampling, although every group has a chance of being selected and included in the sample, there is every possibility, and sometimes it does happen, that certain important groups are left unrepresented. But, in stratified sampling method, no important group is likely to be left out.

Stratified sampling method is the ideal one when comparison between different variables has to be made. For example, if comparison has to be made between men and women teachers, it would be very difficult to select the acquired number of units through any other method of sampling. If any other method is used, the problem of bias and prejudice creeps in.

Replacement of units is also possible in the stratified sampling method. Normally, if a particular unit is not accessible for a study, it is difficult to replace it by another, but in this method it is possible. Stephen states that stratification automatically brings about replacement of persons lost in the sample, by persons of the same stratum, thus partly correcting the bias that would result if there were no replacement of losses. As the entire population is divided into particular strata it is easy and convenient to replace an inaccessible case by an accessible one.

In stratified sampling method, much depends on stratification process. The following precautions were taken while stratifying the population: the variable involved in the study were taken note of, care was taken to see that each stratum in the universe was large enough in size so that selection of items could be done on random basis, the strata formed were definite and clear cut, each stratum was free from influence of the other and there was no overlapping.

Before actually selecting the sample, certain fundamental principles were considered to make the sample scientific and clear-cut.

Firstly, the 'universe' was clearly defined. In the technical phraseology of research, the whole population out of which the samples are selected is known as the 'universe'. For the present research work, the universe includes all the teachers teaching in secondary schools of Andhra Pradesh. The study was limited to a particular geographical area i.e., Guntur district, to facilitate appropriate sample selection and to avoid wastage of time and money.

Secondly, discussion was made about the units of the sample. A unit of sample may be a house, a family, a group of individuals or a single individual. A good unit should possess the following characteristics:

1. ***Clarity:*** The unit should be clearly defined in unambiguous terms. This would make the study easy and efficient. For the present research work, a sampling unit is defined as a teacher teaching in any secondary school of Guntur district.
2. ***Suitability:*** A good unit should be well suited to the problem under study. Since the problem is population education awareness of secondary school teachers, the unit selected is well suited to the problem.
3. ***Accessibility:*** The unit selected should be easily accessible to the researcher. If the units selected are difficult to reach and if he fails to make use of them, the study would be vitiated. The selected sampling unit, i.e. teachers teaching in secondary schools are easily accessible since they could be approached in any secondary school.

Thirdly, availability of sample and preparation of the source list. This is an important factor that makes representative selection possible. A source list is the list which contains the names of the units of the universe from which the sample may be selected. It may exit even before the beginning of the research or it may be prepared afresh by the investigator himself. Without a source list, study through the sampling method is not possible. For the present research work, a source list consisting of the names of secondary schools of Guntur district was used. Care was taken to see that the source list was up-to-date and valid and that there was no repetition of names of the schools. This source list was found to be relevant and suitable because it included the schools as the study deals with the population education awareness of secondary school teachers.

Besides considering these principles it is extremely important to think about the size of the sample to be selected. If the sample is either too small or too large, it will make the study difficult and also make the results untenable. According to Patten, an optimum sample in survey is the one which fulfills the requirements of effective representativeness, reliability and flexibility. The sample should be small enough to avoid intolerable sampling error. The size of the sample for the present research work was decided after considering the following factors.

1. Since a detailed study was planned a very large number of sample was not selected. In case of an intensive study, very large number of sample was not useful as it involves huge consumption of resources. A smaller sample will be convenient.

2. The size and the selection of the samples are also influenced by the nature of the universe. If the universe is homogeneous even a small-sized sample may yield dependable and required results. If the universe is heterogeneous, small-sized samples may not be useful. In case of the present study, the heterogeneous universe was split into smaller homogeneous strata and samples were selected from these strata. For example, the secondary school teachers of Guntur district were broadly grouped under men and women. A sample was selected from each of these two groups.

3. The researchers need to determine the number of the groups to be formed. In case the number of groups proposed is large, the size of the samples shall have to be large so that every group should be of proper size and suit the requirements of the study. In case of the number of groups proposed is small, even small-sized samples can fulfill the requirements. In case of the present study, the number of groups into which the universe was divided were rural and urban, government and private school teachers. Since the number of groups are moderate a reasonable sample was selected from each of these groups.

4. Practical considerations and accuracy will also play a vital role in determining the size of the sample. Every study is guided by certain practical considerations such as time, resources, accessibility of the data, etc. Generally, it is believed that a large-sized sample is more representative and usually produces accurate results. This, of course, mainly depends upon the technique, if the technique is scientific, even small-sized samples can produce dependable and accurate results. For the present study, practical considerations like the availability of resources and time were taken into consideration. Care was taken to make the sample selection technique as scientific as possible.

5. The size of the sample is also governed by the size of the tools to be used. In case the tools are short and the questions asked pertain to certain limited factors, a large sample is required. If the tool is large in size, the sample should be small in size so that, from administrative point of view, the researcher may not be put to unnecessary troubles. In the present study, as the tool is quite elaborate and needs a careful study, hence a very large sample was not selected.

6. The sampling method also determines the size of the sample. When random sampling method is used, the samples have to be large. On the other hand, if

samples are selected through stratified sampling method the reliability can be achieved even with the help of the small-sized samples.

Taking into consideration all these factors which influence the size of the sample, it was decided that an ideal sample would consist of 80 secondary school teachers. This sample is small enough to avoid unnecessary expenditure and large enough to avoid intolerable sampling errors.

After deciding about the sampling method, the population selected was divided into different strata. The variables chosen for the study were considered to divide the population. The sampling design employed involved not only stratification of universe but also the random sampling technique to select samples from within the stratum. The variables chosen were: *(i)* rural versus urban school teachers, *(ii)* private versus government school teachers, and *(iii)* men versus women teachers.

The total sample of 80 secondary school teachers consists of: rural: 40, urban: 40, government school teachers: 40, private school teachers: 40, men teachers: 40, women teachers: 40. The details are given below:

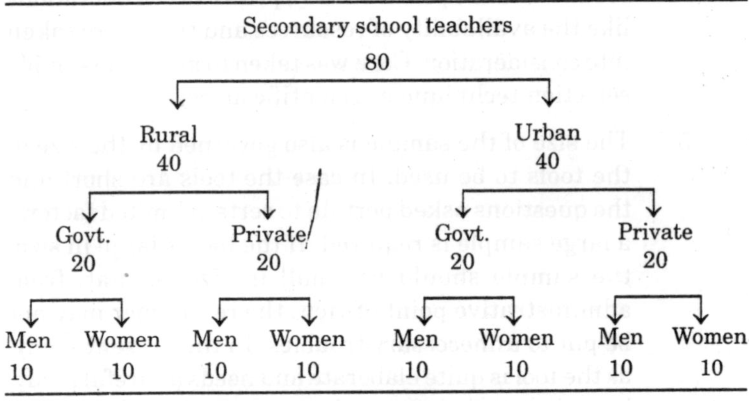

The sampling design employed thus involved not only the stratification of the universe but also the random sampling technique to select samples from within the stratum.

CONSTRUCTION OF RESEARCH TOOL

A research tool plays a major role in any worthwhile research as it is the sole factor in determining the sound data and in arriving at perfect conclusions about the problem or study on hand, which ultimately in providing suitable remedial measures to the problem concerned.

The selection and use of tools can be done in two ways. The first one is to construct a tool independently by the researcher for his own study. Here, there are many problems in doing so on construction of own tools. Anand and Padma felt that a note of caution of caution has to be struck when a researcher develops a tool for his study by merely pooling some items and does not subject it to the sophisticated techniques of tool construction. The result would be then, obviously, a poor quality research. With this, one can say that preparation and standardization of tools is a major task, and one should take care in aspects like selection of area and sample, pooling up of statements related to the area, consulting the experts and application of sophisticated statistical techniques.

The other way of selection and use of tools is right selection of tools from already standardized ones available in the field of study. Here also it involves a tedious job in locating the tools and identifying their usefulness to the study on hand. Even then, this technique is very useful when a research work is taken to study in depth and when the research work involves a good number of variables. Some people believe that some of the instruments available do not measure up to their standards, hence new ones. In some instances, consideration should be given to the logistics of the situation. Lacking time and financial resources for the construction of a test, many researchers cannot expect to produce a better instrument. In these cases, the most logical procedure that one can follow is to choose the best instrument available for this purpose.

Considering the merits and limitations of the selection of research tools in either way, the researcher is interested in using a self-prepared tool as there are no standardized tools suitable to this study. Several statements have been collected from different sources and prepared a rating scale. It was given to experts and administered on a small sample of secondary school teachers. After satisfying thoroughly with the tool construction procedures, the self-prepared tool is named as "Population Education Awareness Scale", which can be used to assess the awareness about population education of secondary school teachers. .

ADMINISTRATION OF THE TOOL

The population education awareness scale was personally administered on a sample of 80 secondary school teachers.

4

Analysis of Data

The organisation, analysis and interpretation of data and formulation of conclusions and generalizations are the next steps after the collection of data to get a meaningful picture out of the raw information collected. The analysis and interpretation of data involves the objective material in the possession of the researcher and his subjective reactions and desires to be derived from the data the inherent meanings in their relation to the problem. (*Rummel*)

The mass data collected through the use of various tools need to be systematized and organised, i.e., edited, classified and tabulated before it can serve the purpose. Here, editing implies the checking of gathered data for accuracy, utility and completeness, classifying refers to the dividing the information into different categories, classes or heads, for use; and tabulating denotes the recording of the classified material in accurate mathematical terms.

The mean scores were used to identify the level of population education awareness possessed by the teachers and to compare the sub-sample variation. The values of standard deviation were used to measure the spread or dispersion of scores in a distribution (Garret, 1979). The critical ratios were calculated to test the significant difference in the means of the two sub-samples of each variable.

To measure the level of awareness about population education possessed by the sample teachers, the total score of population education awareness of each teacher was taken into consideration. The maximum score that a teacher can get was 148 and the minimum score was 52.

Hypothesis—1

"There is no high awareness about population education among secondary school teachers"

To test the validity of the above hypothesis, the mean value was calculated which is given in Table—4.1.

Table—4.1 Level of population education awareness of secondary school teachers

Sample size	*Mean*	*Standard deviation*
80	134.05	7.883

As per the mean value of the value of the total sample, it seems clear that the secondary school teachers are possessing high awareness about population education. The population education awareness scores are normally distributed in the whole sample to a large extent.

The hypothesis that "there is no high awareness about population education among secondary school teachers" is rejected.

Hypothesis—2

"There is no significant difference in the awareness of teachers of rural and urban secondary schools about population education"

To test the validity of the hypothesis 2, the following calculations are made.

Table—4.2 Comparison of the population education awareness of rural and urban secondary school teachers

Variable	Sample size	Mean	Standard deviation	Mean difference	SED	Critical ratio
Rural	40	133.625	7.989			
				0.85	1.755	0.484*
Urban	40	134.475	7.71			

* Not significant at 0.01 level

From the values of Table—4.2, it is evident that there is no significant difference in the possession of awareness about population education by the rural and urban teachers, though both the sub-samples are possessing high awareness about population education awareness.

The hypothesis that "there is no significant difference in the awareness of teachers of rural and urban secondary schools about population education" is accepted.

Hypothesis—3

"There is no significant difference in the awareness of teachers of government and private secondary schools about population education".

The following calculations are made to find out the validity of hypothesis 3.

Table—4.3 Comparison of population education awareness of government and private secondary school teachers

Variable size	Sample	Mean	Standard deviation	Mean difference	SED	Critical ratio
Government	40	135.35	4.942			
				2.55	1.7	1.5*
Private	40	132.8	9.555			

* Not significant at 0.01 level

The teachers working both in government and private secondary schools are possessing high awareness about population education. As per the critical ratio value, there is no significant difference in the level of population education awareness possessed by the teachers working in government and private secondary schools.

The hypothesis that "there is no significant difference in the awareness of teachers of government and private secondary schools about population education" is accepted.

Hypothesis—4

"There is no significant difference in the awareness of men and women teachers about population education".

To test the validity of hypothesis 4, the following calculations are made.

Table—4.4 Comparison of population education awareness of men and women teachers

Variable	*Sample size*	*Mean*	*Standard deviation*	*Mean difference*	*SED*	*Critical Ratio*
Men	40	132.175	7.512			
				3.75	1.745	2.148*
Women	40	135.925	8.091			

* Not significant at 0.01 level

From the mean values of Table—4.4, it seems that the men and women teachers are hold high awareness about population education. As per the critical ratio and value, there is no significant difference in the level of possession of awareness about population education by the two sub-samples.

The hypothesis that "there is no significant difference in the awareness of men and women teachers about population education" is accepted.

5

Summary, Conclusions and Discussion

"A small story about population growth is that there lived many fish in a big pond. In it, there were three big fish, one was *Anagat Vidyana* who was worried about the future and would think about future happenings. The second, *pratyutpannamati*, acted according to the circumstances. The third, *Yada-Bhavishya*, believed in we'll see what happens; why worry now?: When the fisherman arrived there, the first and second fish swam into the adjoining pond, and saved themselves through sheer cleverness and planning. But the third, who cared least for the future, was caught and killed. Liked in this example, shouldn't we worry about the future? Should we shut our eyes to the future, as a pigeon does in the presence of a cat?

Today, the gravest crisis the world faces is the increase in population. There are many problems which are being caused by population like unemployment, shortage of food, etc. Ehbrich in his book 'The Population Bomb' warns that if growth continues at the present rate for 900 years, there would be some sixty million billion people. This would be about 100 persons for each square yard of the earth's surface, land and sea. There is thus an urgent need for taking appropriate measures for arresting population explosion. This is possible only by educating the public. School education has to play a significant role in this sphere. There is thus a need for including a new subject like population education.

Population education is, today, one of the important innovations in the field of education. It has spanned through almost the entire spectrum of school education in a relatively short period and concerted efforts are underway to integrate its elements in other vital sectors of education, namely, non-formal education, adult education and university education. In fact, population education is a need of the hour, if we want to save ourselves from starvation and extinction. Population education, also called "education for population awareness", is of a very recent origin, but gained momentum to a full gear.

As the awareness of population education contributes for the knowledge of general issues of the teachers, the researcher has taken-up a study entitled "A Study of the Awareness about Population Education among Secondary School Teachers" to study the awareness about population education of teachers teaching in the secondary schools of Guntur district.

A summary of the writings of recognised authorities and of previous research, provides sufficient evidence that the research is familiar with what is already known and what is still unknown. It helps to eliminate duplication to fix useful objectives, to form appropriate hypotheses, to draw meaningful conclusions, and to make commendable suggestions. Several important writings on awareness of population and research related to it have been reviewed and incorporated according to their suitability.

The variables chosen for the study were area, management of the school and gender.

Keeping in view the different aspects of the present study the objectives considered were:

1. To find out the awareness of secondary school teachers about population education;

2. To find out the awareness of rural and urban teachers about population education;
3. To find out the awareness of the teachers of government and private secondary schools about population education;
4. To find out the awareness of men and women teachers about population education;

Hypotheses were formulated taking the objectives into consideration. The hypotheses were formulated in null form. The hypotheses formulated were:

1. There is no high awareness about population education among secondary school teachers;
2. There is no significant difference in the awareness of teachers of rural and urban secondary schools about population education;
3. There is no significant difference in the awareness of teachers of government and private secondary schools about population education;
4. There is no significant difference in the awareness of men and women teachers about population education.

Stratified sampling technique was found to be the most appropriate technique because the present study involves the sampling into a good number of groups according to different variables. Through stratified sampling only it is possible to divide the sample into different groups and choose sample from each of the groups. Random sampling technique was also employed to select teachers from each group. Only the secondary school teachers were included for this sampling.

Regarding the size of the sample, 80 may be appropriate. This was found suitable because the study involves through intensity and detail. A sample with more than 80 teachers would involve lot of resources and less than 80 would also bring about problems of representatives. Out of the total sample of 80 secondary school teachers, equal weightage was given to rural and urban teachers, government and private school teachers and men and women teachers.

The research tool occupies a major role in any research study because it is useful in the collection of data to draw meaningful conclusions. The researcher has constructed a rating scale entitled "Population Education Awareness Scale" and used to study the awareness of secondary school teachers about population education.

For the purposes of the analysis of data and deducing the valid conclusions, the statistical techniques like Mean, Standard Deviation, and Critical Ratio were used.

CONCLUSIONS AND DISCUSSION

The following are the conclusions arrived at from the analysis of data.

1. The Secondary School Teachers are having High Awareness About Population Education

The problem of population explosion has been identified by the world after the proposal of Malthus that the population was increasing in geometric progression whereas food production was increasing in arithmetic progression. Ever since the Malthus theory, the governments are trying to reduce the problem of population expecting the future consequences of population explosion, one among them is population education. To make the population education a part of regular curriculum, the curriculum designers made it a hidden part of the curriculum. The teachers were made aware of the population education and its implementation in the schools indirectly. If the teachers are well aware of the population education and its implementation in their classrooms, the population education programme will go ahead with all success. As the secondary school teachers are having high awareness about population education, they have to make their students aware of the benefits and limitations of over population and big family and small family. The teachers with this high awareness about population education should make the members of the society aware about the pros and cons of population explosion as they will be having tremendous influence on the society. They should become models to their students in this area.

2. The Teachers Working in Rural and Urban Secondary Schools are having Equal Awareness About Population Education

Though there may be a significant difference in the exposure of rural and urban teachers to the status of big and small families with regard to wealth, health, education, employment, physical facilities, clothing, food, etc., both rural and urban teachers are having high awareness about population education without any difference between them. Both rural and urban teachers have to bring awareness about population education among their students in order to make the proverb "a small family is a better family" a reality.

3. The Teachers Working in Private and Government Secondary Schools are having Equally High Awareness About Population Education

Many of the educators and public feel that the attitudes of the teachers working in government and private secondary schools differ significantly because of the perks and facilities vary recognizably. Though there is such opinion, the teachers working in private and government secondary schools are having high awareness about population education equally. As these are having high awareness about population education, they should work for a small family norm considering the socio-economic status and other factors associated with the students studying in private and government secondary schools.

4. The Men and Women Teachers Working in Secondary Schools are Possessing Equally High Awareness About Population Education

The men and women teachers with this high awareness about population education should work for the benefits of population education among boys and girls that are exposed to them. If both men and women teachers individually or collectively work for the cause of population education, the gender bias will disappear and an equal status may prevail in both boys and girls.

The secondary school teachers are having high awareness about population education. The locality of the school, the management of the school, and the gender of the teacher are not having any influence on the awareness of population education. As the teachers are holding high awareness about population education, they should try to realize the objectives of population education in their schools.

SUGGESTIONS FOR FURTHER RESEARCH

Based on the enlightenment got from the present study, the following are the studies suggested for further research by the future researchers.

1. Studies may be taken up to study the awareness of primary teachers and college lecturers about population education.
2. Studies may be taken up taking into consideration the variables which were not covered in the present study so as to identify the influence of different kinds of variables on the awareness of the samples about population education.
3. Studies may be taken up with large samples taking the district, state and nation as individual units.
4. Studies may be taken up to identify the relationship between the awareness of teachers and students about population education.

Bibliography

Asha A. Bhende and Tara Kanitkar (1985). *Principles of Population Studies*. Bombay: Himayala Publishing House.

Bhaskara Rao, D., and Damera Sridhar (2003). *Job Satisfaction of School Teachers*. New Delhi: Discovery Publishing House.

Binod Kumar, Sahu (2001). *Population Education*. New Delhi: Sterling Publishers Pvt. Ltd.

Gopal Rao, D. (1981). *A Decade of Population Education Research in India*. New Delhi: NCERT.

Hans, Raj (1984). *Fundamentals of Demography*. New Delhi: Surjeet Publications.

Kuppuswamy, D. (1975). *Population and Society in India*. Bombay: Popular Prakashan Pvt. Ltd.

Mehta, T.S. and Ramachandra (1972). *Population Education: Selected Readings*. New Delhi: NCERT.

Parakh, B.S. (1985). *Population Education—Inspection to Institutionalisation*. New Delhi: NCERT.

Seshadri, C., and Pandey, J.L. (1991). *Population Education: A National Source Book*, Volume 1. New Delhi: NCERT.

Additional Reading

Bhaskara Rao, Digumarti (1994). *Scientific Aptitude*, New Delhi: Ashish Publishing House. ISBN 81-7024-658-X.

Bhaskara Rao, Digumarti (1995). *Animal Kingdom*. New Delhi: Discovery Publishing House. ISBN 81-7141-274-2.

Bhaskara Rao, Digumarti (1995). *Batracology*. New Delhi: Discovery Publishing House. ISBN 81-7141-279-3.

Bhaskara Rao, Digumarti (1996). *Scientific Attitude vis-à-vis Scientific Aptitude*. New Delhi: Discovery Publishing House. ISBN 81-7141-308-0.

Bhaskara Rao, Digumarti (2004). *Scientific Attitude, Scientific Appitude and Achievement*, New Delhi: Discovery Publishing House.

Bhaskara Rao, Digumarti, Editor (1996). *Encyclopaedia of Education for All,* 5 Volumes. New Delhi: APH Publishing Corporation. ISBN 81-7024-759-4 (set).

Vol. I *Education for All: The World Conference*. ISBN 81-7024-760-8.

Vol. II *Education for All: The EPA-9 Summit*. ISBN 81-7024-761-6.

Vol. III *Education for All: Quality Education for All*. ISBN 81-7024-762-6.

Vol. IV *Education for All: Planning and Monitoring*. ISBN 81-7024-763-4.

Vol. V *Education for All: The Indian Scenario*. ISBN 81-7024-764-0.

Bhaskara Rao, Digumarti, Editor (1996). *Global Perceptions on Peace Education*, 3 Volumes. New Delhi: Discovery Publishing House. ISBN 81-7141-319-6.

Bhaskara Rao, Digumarti, Editor (1996). *National Policy on Education*. 2 Volumes. New Delhi: Anmol Publications Pvt. Ltd. ISBN 81-7488-323-1.

Bhaskara Rao, Digumarti, Editor (1997). *Care the Child*, 2 Volumes. New Delhi: Discovery Publishing House. ISBN 81-7141-394-3.

Bhaskara Rao, Digumarti, Editor (1997). *Education for the 21st Century*. New Delhi: Discovery Publishing House. ISBN 81-7141-389-7.

Bhaskara Rao, Digumarti, Editor (1997). *Reflections on Scientific Attitude*. New Delhi: Discovery Publishing House, ISBN 81-7141-319-6.

Bhaskara Rao, Digumarti (1997), *Scientific Attitude*. New Delhi: Discovery Publishing House. ISBN 81-7141-381-1.

Bhaskara Rao, Digumarti, Editor (1997). *Success Story of a Primary Education Project*. New Delhi: APH Publishing Corporation. ISBN 81-7024-850-7.

Bhaskara Rao, Digumarti, Editor (1997). *World Food Summit*. New Delhi: Discovery Publishing House. ISBN 81-7141-386-2.

Bhaskara Rao, Digumarti, Editor (1998). *Adolescence Education*. New Delhi: Discovery Publishing House. ISBN 81-7141-432-X.

Bhaskara Rao, Digumarti, Editor (1998). *Community and School Nutrition Education*. New Delhi: Discovery Publishing House. ISBN 81-7141-435-4.

Bhaskara Rao, Digumarti, Editor (1998). *District Primary Education Programme*. New Delhi: Discovery Publishing House. ISBN 81-7141-396-X.

Bhaskara Rao, Digumarti, Editor (1998). *Earth Summit*, 2 Volumes. New Delhi: Discovery Publishing House. ISBN 81-7141-435-4.

Bhaskara Rao, Digumarti, Editor (1998). *National Policy on Education: Towards an Enlightened and Humane Society*, New Delhi: Discovery Publishing House. ISBN 81-7141-426-5.

Bhaskara Rao, Digumarti, Editor (1998). *Reforming School Education*. New Delhi: Discovery Publishing House. ISBN 81-7141-403-6.

Bhaskara Rao, Digumarti, Editor (1998). *Teacher Education in India*. New Delhi: Discovery Publishing House. ISBN 81-7141-406-0.

Bhaskara Rao, Digumarti, Editor (1998). *World Summit for Social Development*. New Delhi: Discovery Publishing House. ISBN 81-7141-420-6.

Bhaskara Rao, Digumarti, Editor (2000). *Education for All: Achieving the Goal*, 3 Volumes, New Delhi: APH Publishing Corporation. ISBN 81-7648-152-1. (Set)

Vol. I *The Global Consensus*. ISBN 81-7648-153-6.

Vol. II *Mid-Decade Review Reports of Regional Seminars*. ISBN 81-7648-154-8.

Vol. III *Issues and Trends*. ISBN 81-7648-155-6.

Bhaskara Rao, Digumarti, Editor (2000), *International Encyclopaedia of AIDS*, 11 Volumes in 13 Parts. New Delhi: Discovery Publishing House. ISBN 81-7141-6 (Set).

Vol. 1 *Introduction to HIV/AIDS*. ISBN 81-7141-523-7.

Vol. 2 *HIV/AIDS—Issues and Challenges*, 2 Parts. ISBN 81-7141-524-5.

Vol. 3 *HIV/AIDS—Socio Economic Realities*. ISBN 81-7141-525-3.

Vol. 4 *HIV/AIDS—Law Ethics and Human Rights*, 2 Parts. ISBN 81-7141-526-1.

Vol. 5 *AIDS and NGOs*. ISBN 81-7141-527-X.

Vol. 6 *AIDS and Home Care*. ISBN 81-7141-528-8.

Vol. 7 *STD Case Management*. ISBN 81-7141-529-6.

Vol. 8 *HIV/AIDS Prevention and Care—Teaching Modules for Nurses and Midwives*. ISBN 81-7141-530-X.

Vol. 9 *HIV Prevention Education for Educational Institutions*. ISBN 81-7141-531-8.

Vol. 10 *Instructional Modules for AIDS Education*. ISBN 81-7141-532-6.

Vol. 11 *School Health Education to Prevent AIDS and STD—A Package for Curriculum Planners*. ISBN 81-7141-533-4.

Bhaskara Rao, Digumarti, Editor (2000). *International Encyclopaedia of Science and Technology Education*, 11 Volumes. New Delhi: Discovery Publishing House. ISBN 81-7141-548-2 (Set).

Vol. 1 *Science and Technology Education*. ISBN 81-7141-568-7.

Vol. 2 *Science Education in Developing Countries*. ISBN 81-7141-570-9.

Vol. 3 *Organisational Structure of Science*. ISBN 81-7141-570-9.

Vol. 4 *Science Education in Asia and the Pacific*. ISBN 81-7141-571-7.

Vol. 5 *Science and Technology Education for All*. ISBN 81-7141-572-5.

Vol. 6 *Values, Ethics, Talent and Girls in Science and Technology Education*. ISBN 81-7141-573-3.

Vol. 7 *Popularization of Science and Technology Education*. ISBN 81-7141-574-1.

Vol. 8 *Science, Power and Society*. ISBN 81-7141-575-X.

Vol. 9 *Information Technology*. ISBN 81-7141-576-8.

Vol. 10 *Teacher Training in Science and Technology Education*. ISBN 81-7141-577-6.

Vol. 11 *Teacher Training in Science and Technology: A Curriculum Framework*. ISBN 81-7141-578-4.

Bhaskara Rao, Digumarti, Editor (2001). *Distance Education in Different Countries*. New Delhi: APH Publishing Corporation. ISBN 81-7648-229-3.

Bhaskara Rao, Digumarti, Editor (2001). *Decentralised Management of Education (Management of Education in Panchayati Raj and Municipal Bodies)*. New Delhi: Discovery Publishing House. ISBN 81-7141-617-9.

Bhaskara Rao, Digumarti, Editor (2001). *Electrochemistry for Environmental Protection*. New Delhi: Discovery Publishing House. ISBN 81-7141-619-5.

Bhaskara Rao, Digumarti, Editor (2001). *Global Educational Studies*. New Delhi: Discovery Publishing House. ISBN 81-7141-616-0.

Bhaskara Rao, Digumarti, Editor (2001). *Global Synthesis of Educational Assessment*. New Delhi: Discovery Publishing House. ISBN 81-7141-613-6.

Bhaskara Rao, Digumarti, Editor (2000). *International Encyclopaedia of Human Rights*. 7 Volumes in 13 Parts. New Delhi: Discovery Publishing House. ISBN 81-7141-567-9 (Set).

Vol. 1 *International Instruments of Human Rights,* 2 Parts. ISBN 81-7141-595-4.

Vol. 2 *Regional Instruments of Human Rights*. ISBN 81-7141-604-7.

Vol. 3 *Human Rights and the United Nations,* 2 Parts. ISBN 81-7141-605-5.

Vol. 4 *Fact Files of Human Rights,* 3 Parts. ISBN 81-7141-605-3.

Vol. 5 *Study Stories of Human Rights,* 3 Parts. ISBN 81-7141-607-3.

Vol. 6 *International Meetings on Human Rights,* 2 Parts. ISBN 81-7141-608-X.

Vol. 7 *Professional Training in Human Rights*. ISBN 81-7141-609-8.

Bhaskara Rao, Digumarti, Editor (2001). *Jomtein Decade of Education*. New Delhi: Discovery Publishing House. ISBN 81-7141-618-7.

Bhaskara Rao, Digumarti, Editor (2001). *Nuclear Materials: Issues and Concerns*, 2 Volumes. New Delhi: Discovery Publishing House. ISBN 81-7141-611-X.

Bhaskara Rao, Digumarti, Editor (2001). *World Conference on Education for All*. New Delhi: APH Publishing Corporation. ISBN 81-7648-274-9.

Bhaskara Rao, Digumarti, Editor (2001). *World Conference on Higher Education*, New Delhi: Discovery Publishing House. ISBN 81-7141-610-1.

Bhaskara Rao, Digumarti, Editor (2001). *World Conference on Science*. New Delhi: Discovery Publishing House. ISBN 81-7141-612-8.

Bhaskara Rao, Digumarti, Editor (2003). *Inspiring Experience in Teacher Education*. New Delhi: Discovery Publishing House. ISBN 81-7141-656-X.

Bhaskara Rao, Digumarti, Editor (2003). *International Studies in Education*, 3 Volumes, New Delhi: Discovery Publishing House. ISBN 81-7141-647-0. (Set)

Bhaskara Rao, Digumarti, Editor (2003). *Military Conversion: Impact on Science and Technology*, New Delhi: Discovery Publishing House. ISBN 81-7141-578-4.

Bhaskara Rao, Digumarti, Editor (2003). *United Nations Millennium Summit*. New Delhi: Discovery Publishing House. ISBN 81-7141-632-2.

Bhaskara Rao, Digumarti, Editor (2003). *World Assembly on Aging*. New Delhi: Discovery Publishing House. ISBN 81-7141-637-3.

Bhaskara Rao, Digumarti, Editor (2003). *World Conference on Human Rights*. New Delhi: Discovery Publishing House. ISBN 81-7141-661-6.

Bhaskara Rao, Digumarti, Editor (2003). *World Education Forum*. New Delhi: Discovery Publishing House. ISBN 81-7141-639-X.

Bhaskara Rao, Digumarti, Editor (2003). *Education Employment and Human Resource Development*. New Delhi: Discovery Publishing House. ISBN 81-7141-681-0.

Bhaskara Rao, Digumarti, Editor (2004). *Learning to Live Together*, 4 Volumes, New Delhi: Discovery Publishing House.

Bhaskara Rao, Digumarti, Editor (2003). *Successful Schooling*. New Delhi: Discovery Publishing House. ISBN 81-7141-677-2.

Bhaskara Rao, Digumarti, Editor (2004). *European Education and Teachers*. New Delhi: Discovery Publishing House. ISBN 81-7141-702-7.

Bhaskara Rao, Digumarti, Editor (2003). *Teachers in a Changing World*. New Delhi: Discovery Publishing House. ISBN 81-7141-694-2.

Bhaskara Rao, Digumarti, Editor, (2003). *Education: Policies and Programmes,* New Delhi: APH Publishing Corporation. ISBN 81-7648-470-9.

Bhaskara Rao, Digumarti, C.A.P. Swami and B.S.V. Dutt (1997). *Self-Evaluation in Student Teaching*. New Delhi: Discovery Publishing House. ISBN 81-7141-374-9.

Bhaskara Rao, Digumarti and Digumarti Pushpa Latha (1994). *Achievement in Biology*. New Delhi: Discovery Publishing House. ISBN 81-7141-264-5.

Bhaskara Rao, Digumarti, C. Sridevi and K. Vijaya (1995). *Achievement in Social Studies*. New Delhi: Discovery Publishing House. ISBN 81-7141-281-5.

Bhaskara Rao, Digumarti and Digumarti Pushpa Latha (1995). *Achievement in English*. New Delhi: Discovery Publishing House. ISBN 81-7141-283-1.

Bhaskara Rao, Digumarti and Digumarti Pushpa Latha (1994). *Achievement in Science*. New Delhi: Discovery Publishing House. ISBN 81-7141-280-70.

Bhaskara Rao, Digumarti and Digumarti Pushpa Latha (1995). *Achievement in Mathematics*. New Delhi: Discovery Publishing House. ISBN 81-7141-278-5.

Bhaskara Rao, Digumarti and Digumarti Pushpa Latha, Editors (1998). *International Encyclopaedia of Women*. 5 Volumes. New Delhi: Discovery Publishing House. ISBN 81-7141-410-9.

Vol. 1 *Status of World's Women*. ISBN 81-7141-494-X.

Vol. 2 *Women, Education and Empowerment*. ISBN 81-7141-498-1.

Vol. 3 *Women Challenges and Advancement*. ISBN 81-7141-497-4.

Vol. 4 *Women and Family Health*. ISBN 81-7141-497-4.

Vol. 5 *Women and International Action*. ISBN 81-7141-498-2.

Bhaskara Rao, Digumarti, Digumarti Pushpa Latha and Digumarti Harshitha, Editors (2001). *Biological Warfare*. New Delhi: Discovery Publishing House. ISBN 81-7141-597-0.

Bhaskara Rao, Digumarti, Digumarti Pushpa Latha and Digumarti Harshitha, Editors (2001). *Women as Educators*. New Delhi: Discovery Publishing House. ISBN 81-7141-602-0.

Bhaskara Rao, Digumarti and Digumarti Harshitha, Editors (2001). *Education in India*. New Delhi: APH Publishing Corporation. ISBN 81-7648-207-2.

Bhaskara Rao, Digumarti, Digumarti Pushpa Latha and Digumarti Harshitha, Editors (2001). *Assessing Learning Achievement*. New Delhi: Discovery Publishing House. ISBN 81-7141-601-2.

Bhaskara Rao, Digumarti, Digumarti Pushpa Latha and Digumarti Harshitha, Editors (2001). *Energy Security*. New Delhi: Discovery Publishing House. ISBN 81-7141-598-9.

Bhaskara Rao, Digumarti, Digumarti Harshitha and K.R.S.S. Rao, Editors (1999). *Advanced Biotechnology*. New Delhi: Discovery Publishing House. ISBN 81-7141-516-4.

Bhaskara Rao, Digumarti and D. Sridhar (2002). *Job Satisfaction of School Teachers*. New Delhi: Discovery Publishing House. ISBN 81-7141-652-7.

Bhaskara Rao, Digumarti and K.R.S. Sambhasiva Rao, Editors (1996). *Current Trends in Indian Education*. New Delhi: Discovery Publishing House. ISBN 81-7141-311-0.

Bhaskara Rao, Digumarti and K. Vijaya (1995). *A Text Book of Evaluation*. Ambala Cantt: The Associated Publishers.

Bhaskara Rao, Digumarti and N.V.M. Mohana Rao (2002). *Problems of Mentally Handicapped Children*. New Delhi: Discovery Publishing House. ISBN 81-7141-645-4.

Bhaskara Rao, Digumarti and S. Chandra Mohan (2002). *Sports Management*. New Delhi: APH Publishing Corporation. ISBN 81-7648-467-9.

Bhaskara Rao, Digumarti, V.V. Rao, V.V. Lakshmi and V.V. Krishna, Editors (1999). *Status and Advancement of Women*. New Delhi: APH Publishing Corporation. ISBN 81-7648-169-6.

Babu, P.C., Author and Digumarti Bhaskara Rao, Editor (2004). *Flowers of Wisdom*, New Delhi: Discovery Publishing House. ISBN 81-7141-695-0.

Bhagya Lakshmi, Lingineni, Author and Digumarti Bhaskara Rao, Editor (2000). *Reading and Comprehension*. New Delhi: Discovery Publishing House. ISBN 81-7141-543-1.

Bhuvaneswara Lakshmi, Gadde, Author and Digumarti Bhaskara Rao, Editor (2000). *Attitude Towards Science*. New Delhi: Discovery Publishing House. ISBN 81-7141-541-6.

Devraj, T.A.S., Author and Digumarti Bhaskara Rao, Editor (1997). *Trace Analysis of Uranium and Thorium*. New Delhi: Discovery Publishing House. ISBN 81-7141-375-7.

Durga Rani, K., Author and Digumarti Bhaskara Rao, Editor (2000). *Educational Aspirations and Scientific Attitudes* New Delhi: Discovery Publishing House. ISBN 81-7141-555-55.

Dutt, B.S.V. and Digumarti Bhaskara Rao (2001). *Empowering Primary Teachers*. New Delhi: Discovery Publishing House. ISBN 81-7141-615-2.

Ediger, Marlow and Digumarti Bhaskara Rao (1996). *Science Curriculum*. New Delhi: Discovery Publishing House. ISBN 81-7141-321-8.

Ediger, Marlow and Digumarti Bhaskara Rao (2000). *Teaching Mathematics Successfully*. New Delhi: Discovery Publishing House. ISBN 81-7141-552-0.

Ediger, Marlow and Digumarti Bhaskara Rao (2001). *Teaching Science Successfully*. New Delhi: Discovery Publishing House. ISBN 81-7141-600-4.

Ediger, Marlow and Digumarti Bhaskara Rao (2001). *Teaching Social Studies Successfully*. New Delhi: Discovery Publishing House. ISBN 81-7141-596-2.

Ediger, Marlow and Digumarti Bhaskara Rao (2002). *Philosophy and Curriculum*. New Delhi: Discovery Publishing House. ISBN 81-7141-631-4.

Ediger, Marlow and Digumarti Bhaskara Rao (2002). *Improving School Administration*. New Delhi: Discovery Publishing House. ISBN 81-7141-633-0.

Ediger, Marlow and Digumarti Bhaskara Rao (2002). *Elementary Curriculum*. New Delhi: Discovery Publishing House. ISBN 81-7141-658-6.

Ediger, Marlow and Digumarti Bhaskara Rao (2003), *Psychology and Curriculum*. New Delhi: Discovery Publishing House. ISBN 81-7141-691-8.

Ediger, Marlow and Digumarti Bhaskara Rao (2003). *Language Arts Curriculum*. New Delhi: Discovery Publishing House. ISBN 81-7141-657-8.

Ediger, Marlow and Digumarti Bhaskara Rao (2003). *Teaching Language Arts Successfully*. New Delhi: Discovery Publishing House.

Ediger, Marlow and Digumarti Bhaskara Rao (2003). *Teaching Mathematics in Elementary Schools*. New Delhi: Discovery Publishing House. ISBN 81-7141-687-X.

Ediger, Marlow and Digumarti Bhaskara Rao (2003). *Teaching Science in Elementary Schools*. New Delhi: Discovery Publishing House. ISBN 81-7141-698-5.

Ediger, Marlow and Digumarti Bhaskara Rao, (2004). *Teaching Social Studies in Elementary Schools*. New Delhi: Discovery Publishing House.

Ediger, Marlow and Digumarti Bhaskara Rao (2003). *School Curriculum and Administration*. New Delhi: Discovery Publishing House. ISBN 81-7141-709-4.

Ediger, Marlow and Digumarti Bhaskara Rao (2004): *Relevancy in Elementary Curriculum*. New Delhi: Discovery Publishing House. ISBN 81-7141-751-5.

Ediger Marlow, B.S.V. Dutt and Digumarti Bhaskara Rao (2004). *Teaching English Successfully*. New Delhi: Discovery Publishing House. ISBN 81-7141-707-8.

Jayasree, Kandi, Author and Digumarti Bhaskara Rao, Editor (1999). *Correlates of Socialisation*. New Delhi: Discovery Publishing House. ISBN 81-7141-517-2.

John Babu, Chikati, Author and T.J.R. Prasad, G.M. Madhukar and Digumarti Bhaskara Rao, Editors (1996). *Problem Solving in Mathematics*. New Delhi: APH Publishing Corporation. ISBN 81-7648-273-0.

Jyothi Nirmala, M., Author and Digumarti Bhaskara Rao, Editor (2003). *Non-detention Systems in School Education*. New Delhi: Discovery Publishing House. ISBN 81-7141-654-3.

Marja, Talvi and Digumarti Bhaskara Rao, Editors (1996). *Educational Leadership and Social Changes*. New Delhi: Discovery Publishing House. ISBN 81-7141-320-X.

Prabhakaram, K.S., Author and Digumarti Bhaskara Rao, Editor (1998). *Concept Attainment Model in Mathematics Teaching*. New Delhi: Discovery Publishing House. ISBN 81-7141-424-9.

Prasanth Kumar, J., Author and Digumarti Bhaskara Rao, Editor (1998). *Effectiveness of Distance Education System*. New Delhi: Discovery Publishing House. ISBN 81-7141-437-0.

Prasanth Kumar, J., Author and G. Sundara Rao and Digumarti Bhaskara Rao, Editors (2000). *Open University Student Support Services*. New Delhi: Discovery Publishing House. ISBN 81-7141-550-4.

Ramkumar Ratnam, M., Author and Digumarti Bhaskara Rao, Editor (2003). *Dukka: Suffering in Early Buddhism*. New Delhi: Discovery Publishing House. ISBN 81-7141-653-4.

Ramatulasamma, K., Author and Digumarti Bhaskara Rao, Editor (2002). *Job Satisfaction of Teacher Educators*, New Delhi: Discovery Publishing House. ISBN 81-7141-655-1.

Rama Krishnaiah, D., Author and Digumarti Bhaskara Rao, Editor (1998). *Job Satisfaction of College Teachers*, New Delhi: Discovery Publishing House. ISBN 81-7141-438-9.

Rathaiah, Lavu and Digumarti Bhaskara Rao, Editors (1996). *International Innovations in Education*. New Delhi: Discovery Publishing House. ISBN 81-7141-359-5.

Ramesh, Ganta and Digumarti Bhaskara Rao, Editors (1998). *Environmental Education: Problems and Prospects*. New Delhi: Discovery Publishing House. ISBN 81-7141-423-0.

Rathaiah, Lavu and Digumarti Bhaskara Rao (1997). *Achievement Correlates*. New Delhi: Discovery Publishing House. ISBN 81-7141-385-4.

Reddy, Sudhakar Y., Author, and Digumarti Bhaskara Rao, Editor (2003). *Creativity in Adolescents*. New Delhi: Discovery Publishing House. ISBN 81-7141-659-4.

Reddy, M.S., Author and Digumarti Bhaskara Rao, Editor (2003). *Creativity in College Students*. New Delhi: Discovery Publishing House. ISBN 81-7141-697-7.

Radramamba, B., Author and Digumarti Bhaskara Rao, Editor (2003). *Problems of Teaching*. New Delhi: APH Publishing Corporation. ISBN 81-7648-462-8.

Sanjeeva Rao, P.C., Author and Digumarti Bhaskara Rao, Editor (1996). *A Text Book of Geology*. New Delhi: Discovery Publishing House. ISBN 81-7141-313-7.

Satya Narayana V., Author and Digumarti Bhaskara Rao, Editor (2001). *Physical Education, Social Attitudes and Leadership Qualities*. New Delhi: Discovery Publishing House. ISBN 81-7141-593-8.

Srinivasulu Reddy, M., and K.R.S. Sambasiva Rao, Authors and Digumarti Bhaskara Rao, Editor (1999). *A Text Book of Aquaculture*. New Delhi: Discovery Publishing House. ISBN 81-7141-482-6.

Srinivasa Reddy, M., and K.R.S. Sambasiva Rao, Authors and Digumarti Bhaskara Rao, Editor (1999). *A Textbook of Aquaculture*. New Delhi: Discovery Publishing House. ISBN 81-7141-482-6.

Vanaja, M., N.S. Latha and Digumarti Bhaskara Rao, (2003), *Student Shyness*, New Delhi: APH Publishing Corporation. ISBN 81-7648-545-4.

Vanaja, M. Author and Digumarti Bhaskara Rao, Editor (1999). *Inquiry Training Model*. New Delhi: Discovery Publishing House. ISBN 81-7141-515-6.

Valeri V. Koustiouk, Author and Digumarti Bhaskara Rao, Editor (2002). *A Text Book of Cryogenics*. New Delhi: Discovery Publishing House. ISBN 81-7141-642-X.

Veena Kumari, Balusu and Digumarti Bhaskara Rao (1996). *Operation Black Board*. New Delhi: Ashish Publishing Corporation.

Veena Kumari, Balusu, Author and Digumarti Bhaskara Rao, Editor (2000). *Psycho-Social Correlates of Achievement*, New Delhi: Discovery Publishing House. ISBN 81-7141-547-4.

Venkata Rao, P. and Digumarti Bhaskara Rao (1989). *A Text Book of Zoology—Junior Intermediate*. Guntur: Vignan Publishers.

Venkata Rao, P. and Digumarti Bhaskara Rao (1989). *A Text Book of Zoology—Senior Intermediate*. Guntur: Vignan Publishers.

Venugopala Rao, K., Author and Digumarti Bhaskara Rao, Editor (2000). *Teacher Morale in Secondary Schools*. New Delhi: Discovery Publishing House. ISBN 81-7141-551-2.

Vidya, C., Author and Digumarti Bhaskara Rao. Editor (1996). *A Text Book of Nutrition*. New Delhi: Discovery Publishing House. ISBN 81-7141-309-9.

Vidya Bharathi, D., Author and Digumarti Bhaskara Rao, Editor (2000). *Educational Philosophies of Swami Vivekananda and John Dewey*. New Delhi: APH Publishing Corporation. ISBN 81-7648-309-9.

Books in Telugu Language

Bhaskara Rao, Digumarti (1986). *Dhrushya Sravana Bodhanapakaranalu* (Audio Visual Teaching Aids). Guntur: Nagarjuna Publishers.

Bhaskara Rao, Digumarti (1993). *Jeevasashtra Bodhana* (Teaching of Biology). Guntur: Nagarjuna Publishers.

Bhaskara Rao, Digumarti (1995). *Vignanasasthra Bodhana* (Teaching of Science) Guntur: Nagarjuna Publishers.

Bhaskara Rao, Digumarti (1997). *Vidya Manovignana Seshtram* (Educational Psychology). Guntur: Creative Press.

Bhaskara Rao, Digumarti (1998). *DSC Study Material*. Guntur: Nagarjuna Publishers.

Bhaskara Rao, Digumarti (1998). *Upadhyayudu Vidya*. (Teacher and Education). Guntur: Nagarjuna Publishers.

Bhaskara Rao, Digumarti (1998). *Vidya Drukpadalu* (Prespectives of Education). Guntur: Nagarjuna Publishers.

Bhaskara Rao, Digumarti (1999). *EdCET Teaching Aptitude*. Guntur: Nagarjuna Publishers.

Bhaskara Rao, Digumarti (2001). *Bharata Samajamulo Upadyayudu Vidya* (Teacher and Education in Emerging Indian Society). Guntur: Nagarjuna Publishers.

Bhaskara Rao, Digumarti (2001). *Bhoutika Sastra Bodhana Paddathulu* (Methods of Teaching Physical Science). Guntur: Nagarjuna Publishers.

Bhaskara Rao, Digumarti (2001). *Jeeva Sastra Bodhana Padhathulu* (Methods of Teaching Biology). Guntur: Nagarjuna Publishers.

Bhaskara Rao, Digumarti (2001). *Vidya Manovignana Sastram* (Educational Psychology). Guntur: Nagarjuna Publishers.

Bhaskara Rao, Digumarti (2003). *Patsala Yajamanyam / Paripalana* (School Management and Administration). Guntur: Nagarjuna Publishers.

Bhaskara Rao, Digumarti (2004). *Vidya Sanketika Sastram-mariyu Computer Vidya* (Educational Technology and Computer Education). Guntur: Nagarjuna Publishers.

Index

A

Achievement of aims, 15
AIDS, 20
Anagal Vidyana, 55
Awareness of teachers, 56-57, 58-60

B

Balasubromaniam, 29

C

China, 10
Comparison of population education awareness of government and private secondary school teachers, 53
men and women teachers, 54
rural and urban secondary school teachers, 53
Components of population education, 13
consequences of population growth, 13
determinants of population growth, 13
population control, 13
Criteria for suitable teachers, 16
Curriculum, 15, 16-17, 28, 29
– of population education, 16
curriculum at the primary stage, 16-19
demographic implication, 19
economic life, 17
education life, 19
environment, 17-18
family life, 18
health, 18
nutrition, 18-19
social life, 17
curriculum at the secondary stage
demographic implication, 20
economic life, 20
environment life, 21
family life, 21
sex life, 20-21
social life, 19

D

Dayal, Shailbala, 33
Definitions, 9
Deforestation, 5

E

Educational implication, 5

F

Family planning programme, 1, 10, 11, 23, 40
Fertility behaviour, 3, 10, 11

G

Gandhi, Indira, 11

Guntur district, 5

H

Hypothesis of the study, 42-43

K

Knodel, John, 3
Korea, 11

L

Level of population education awareness of secondary school teachers, 52

M

Maheswari, J.R., 31
Malthus, 1, 4
Mehta, Ganesh Lal, 34
Men and women teacher working in secondary schools, 59

N

Nagda, S.L., 35
National population education projects, 14
NCERT, 9
Need for population education, 10

O

Operational definitions of key terms, 40
government schools, 41
population growth, 40-41
private schools, 41
rural schools, 41
urban schools, 41

P

Population change, 10
– education, 2, 3, 5, 9, 12
Awareness Scale, 50
consequences, 13
curriculum, 15
determinants, 13
integration, 23
issues, 22
objectives, 13-15
perception, 22
purpose, 22
secondary teacher's training level, 24
– growth, 3, 7
– problem, 2
Prachualmoh, Visid, 3
Pratyutpannamati, 55
Problems of growth rate of population, 7-8

R

Ramachandran, 36
Rao, D. Gopal, 9, 38
Rao, V.K.R.V., 14
Reflects trends in education, 16
Rummel, 51
Rural women, 11

S

Secondary school teachers, 58
Selection of sample, 43
Selection of suitable methods, 16
Sex education, 20, 30
Srivastava, N.N., 32
Statement of the problem, 4

T

Teacher's role in population education, 24
Teachers, 56-60
– working in private and government secondary schools, 59

– – – rural and urban secondary schools, 59
Teaching methodologies, 26
classroom teaching, 26
creative writings among teachers, 27
display of posters, 27
extra model lectures, 26
film shows, 27
organisation of co-curricular activities, 27
visit and field trips, 27
wall magazine, 27
Textbooks, 28
Thakore, Rashmin, 39
Theory of population, 1

U

UNESCO, 9
Urban women, 3, 11

V

Varghese, P.V., 30
Variables of the study, 41-42
government versus private school teachers, 42
men versus women teachers, 42
rural versus urban school teachers, 42
Vaswani, N.C., 38
Veiderman, Stephen, 9, 12

Y

Yada Bhavishya, 55